SHORT WALKS IN THE SURREY HILLS

by Nike Werstroh and Jacint Mig

CICERONE

The wide paths of the Denbies estate are easy to follow (Walk 11)

CONTENTS

USING THIS GUIDE

Routes in this book

In this book you will find a selection of easy or moderate walks suitable for almost everyone, including casual walkers and families with children, or for when you only have a short time to fill. The routes have been carefully chosen to allow you to explore the area and its attractions. Most routes are circular, although some linear walks may be included that use public transport to get back to the start. Although there may be some climbs there is no challenging terrain, but do bear in mind that conditions can sometimes be wet or muddy underfoot. A route summary table is included on page 6 to help you choose the right walk.

Clothing and footwear

You won't need any special equipment to enjoy these walks. The weather in Britain can be changeable, so choose clothing suitable for the season and wear or carry a waterproof jacket. For footwear, comfortable walking boots or trainers with a good grip are best. A small rucksack for drinks, snacks and spare clothing is useful. See www.adventuresmart.uk.

Walk descriptions

At the beginning of each walk you'll find all the information you need:

- start/finish location, with postcode and a what3words address to help you find it
- parking and transport information, estimated walking time, total distance and climb
- details of public toilets available along the route and where you can get refreshments
- a summary of the key highlights of the walk and what you might see

Timings given are the time to complete the walk at a reasonable walking pace. Allow extra time for extended stops or if walking with children.

The route is described in clear, easy-to-follow directions, with each waypoint marked on an accompanying map extract. It's a good idea to read the whole of the route instructions before setting out, so that you know what to expect.

Maps, GPX files and what3words

Extracts from the OS 1:25,000 map accompany each route. GPX files for all the walks in this book are available to download at www.cicerone.co.uk/1153/gpx.

What3words is a free smartphone app which identifies every 3m square of the globe with a unique three-word address, e.g. ///destiny.cafe.sonic. For more information see https://what3words.com/products/what3words-app.

Walking with children

Even young children can be surprisingly strong walkers, but every family is different and you may need to adapt the timings given in this book to take that into account. Make sure you go at the pace of the slowest member and choose a walk with an exciting objective in mind, such as a cave, waterfall or picnic spot. Many of the walks can be shortened to suit – suggestions are included at the end of the route description.

Dogs

Sheep or cattle may be found grazing on a number of these walks. Keep dogs under control at all times so that they don't scare or disturb livestock or wildlife. Cattle, particularly cows with calves, may very occasionally pose a risk to walkers with dogs. If you ever feel threatened by cattle, you should let go of your dog's lead and let it run free.

Enjoying the countryside responsibly

Enjoy the countryside and treat it with respect to protect our natural environments. Stick to footpaths and take your litter home with you. When driving, slow down on rural roads and park considerately, or better still use public transport. For more details check out www.gov.uk/countryside-code.

The Countryside Code

Respect everyone
- be considerate to those living in, working in and enjoying the countryside
- leave gates and property as you find them
- do not block access to gateways or driveways when parking
- be nice, say hello, share the space
- follow local signs and keep to marked paths unless wider access is available

Protect the environment
- take your litter home – leave no trace of your visit
- do not light fires and only have BBQs where signs say you can
- always keep dogs under control and in sight
- dog poo – bag it and bin it – any public waste bin will do
- care for nature – do not cause damage or disturbance

Enjoy the outdoors
- check your route and local conditions
- plan your adventure – know what to expect and what you can do
- enjoy your visit, have fun, make a memory

ROUTE SUMMARY TABLE

WALK NAME	START POINT	TIME	DISTANCE
1. Tilford and Frensham Little Pond	Tilford East Bridge	2¼hr	8km (5 miles)
2. Crooksbury Hill and Waverley Abbey	Waverley Abbey House	2hr	6.5km (3¾ miles)
3. Devil's Punch Bowl	Devil's Punch Bowl, Hindhead	2½hr	8km (5 miles)
4. Guildford and the River Wey	Town Bridge, Guildford	2hr	7km (4¼ miles)
5. St Martha's Hill and Chilworth Gunpowder Mills	Chantries car park	3hr	8km (5 miles)
6. Bramley old railway and the River Wey	Bramley	2½hr	8km (5 miles)
7. Newlands Corner and Silent Pool	Newlands Corner	2½hr	8km (5 miles)
8. Shere woodlands	Shere	1¾hr	5km (3 miles)
9. Hurtwood and Holmbury Hill	Peaselake	2½hr	8km (5 miles)
10. The Lovelace Bridges	Green Dene car park	2hr	6.5km (4 miles)
11. Denbies Hillside and vineyard	Dorking railway station	2hr	6km (3¾ miles)
12. Box Hill and the Stepping Stones	Box Hill and Westhumble railway station	1½hr	4.5km (2¾ miles)
13. Box Hill Hike	Box Hill	4hr	12.5km (7¾ miles)
14. Leith Hill	Coldharbour	2hr	6km (3¾ miles)
15. Reigate Fort	Reigate railway station	2½hr	8km (5 miles)

HIGHLIGHTS
Medieval bridge and pond, river
Views and ruined abbey
Views and history
Views and chapel ruins, river
Views and remains of mill
River and woodlands
Views, pond and gin distillery
Charming village, woodlands
Views and iron age fort
Historic bridges and woodlands
Views and vineyard
Views, history
Views, history, woodlands
Tower and views, woodlands
Views and fort

SYMBOLS USED ON ROUTE MAPS

(S) Start point

(F) Finish point

(SF) Start and finish at the same place

[4]→ Waypoint

~ Route line

MAPPING IS SHOWN AT A SCALE OF 1:25,000

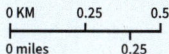

0 KM 0.25 0.5
0 miles 0.25

DOWNLOADED THE GPX FILES FOR FREE AT
www.cicerone.co.uk/1153/GPX

Find a charming pub for a lunch or refreshment

INTRODUCTION

The south-facing slopes of the Surrey Hills are ideal for growing grapes (Walk 11)

Less than an hour from the bustle of London you will find England's most densely wooded county, Surrey. A rich mosaic of farmland, woodland, heathland, downs, commons and rivers make up this diverse landscape. The rolling Surrey Hills that cover a quarter of the county have been designated an Area of Outstanding Natural Beauty (AONB) since 1958. Not surprisingly, writers such as Jane Austen, CS Lewis, Charles Dickens and Lewis Carroll were all inspired by the beautiful scenery of Surrey. The landscape has also provided a backdrop for many scenes in numerous movies.

This relatively small area has lots to offer for outdoor lovers. The narrow roads that connect the villages attract cyclists, and mountain bikers use some of the bridleways in the woodlands. Narrowboats slowly navigate through the locks and kayakers enjoy the River Wey all year round. Meanwhile the extensive network of paths in the dense woodland provides endless routes for walking and running. The Surrey Hills may not be high, but numerous vantage points offer some surprisingly fine views.

The wooded slopes and the heathlands are important habitat for a variety of wildlife, but it is the human hand that has shaped and used the landscape for thousands of years. There is evidence of iron age forts and as you follow the trails, you will sooner or later stumble upon a WW2 pillbox or a fort that was part of the 19th-century defence line. Other historical sights to be seen as you follow the walks in this book include old chapels, medieval bridges, a disused railway line, and an historic gunpowder mill. More modern features include vineyards and a gin distillery.

Walking in the Surrey Hills

From leisurely riverside walks to afternoon strolls in leafy woodlands, from panoramic views to hidden history, walking is the best way to explore the Surrey Hills. The walks in this book can be enjoyed all year round through the changing seasons. In spring bluebells carpet the forest floor and during the summer months the woodland is myriad shades of green. Autumn dresses the trees in spectacular colours and on crisp winter days, you can enjoy far-reaching views from the hills.

The wooded Surrey Hills are criss-crossed with a network of bridleways and public footpaths that are used and enjoyed by walkers, runners and dog walkers. Many of the walks described in this book also make use of the long-distance North Downs Way that traverses the rolling chalk hills, heathlands, pastures and woodlands, visiting some of the iconic beauty spots along the way. Allow time to stop for a picnic or finish your walk with a drink in a cosy pub in one of the historic market towns or charming villages.

Things to see

With good train and bus links from London it is easy to explore Surrey. Follow one of the well-trodden popular paths to Box Hill (Walks 12 and 13), Leith Hill (Walk 14) or Holmbury Hill (Walk 9) for great views. Stroll the

Far-reaching views from Newlands Corner (Walk 7)

The Wey and the Mole are the main rivers in Surrey

streets of the charming village of Sheer (Walk 8) or explore the county town of Guildford (Walk 4). Only a short walk from Guildford town centre you find St Catherine's Hill with a 14-century chapel ruin (Walk 4) or St Martha's Hill with a church (Walk 5).

Travel

The attractive towns and villages in Surrey offer a slower pace of life while still remaining well connected with London. There are frequent train services to Guildford and Dorking and most of the trails in the Surrey Hills are easily accessible from the capital for a pleasant day out. The major towns can be reached by train and many of the villages mentioned in the book are served by buses. The walks in this book are all circular. There are, however, a few that start from a car park outside of towns and villages and if you don't have your own transport you might have to arrange a short taxi or Uber ride to the start.

Where to stay

If you want to spend a couple of days in the area there are places to stay in Guildford, Dorking and Farnham, and there are inns in some of the villages. If you would prefer something different, there are plenty of privately rented rooms and cottages to be found on airbnb.

Crossing the River Wey

WALK 1
Tilford and Frensham Little Pond

Start/finish	*Tilford East Bridge*
Locate	*GU10 2BU ///cashier.stickler.messaging*
Cafes/pubs	*Pub in Tilford, cafe by Frensham Little Pond*
Transport	*Take Tilford Road from Farnham. Bus from Farnham to Charles Hill (B3001) 2km from the start*
Parking	*Tilford Green car park*
Toilets	*No public toilets available*

Time: 2¼hr
Distance: 8km (5 miles)
Climb: 95m

A gentle woodland walk with a visit to a tranquil heathland pond

From the medieval bridge in Tilford this walk wanders through woodland to Frensham Little Pond. You can picnic on the sandy shore or extend the trail and walk around the pond. Return to Tilford alongside the river and treat yourself to a drink in the old pub on the village green.

Medieval bridge in Tilford

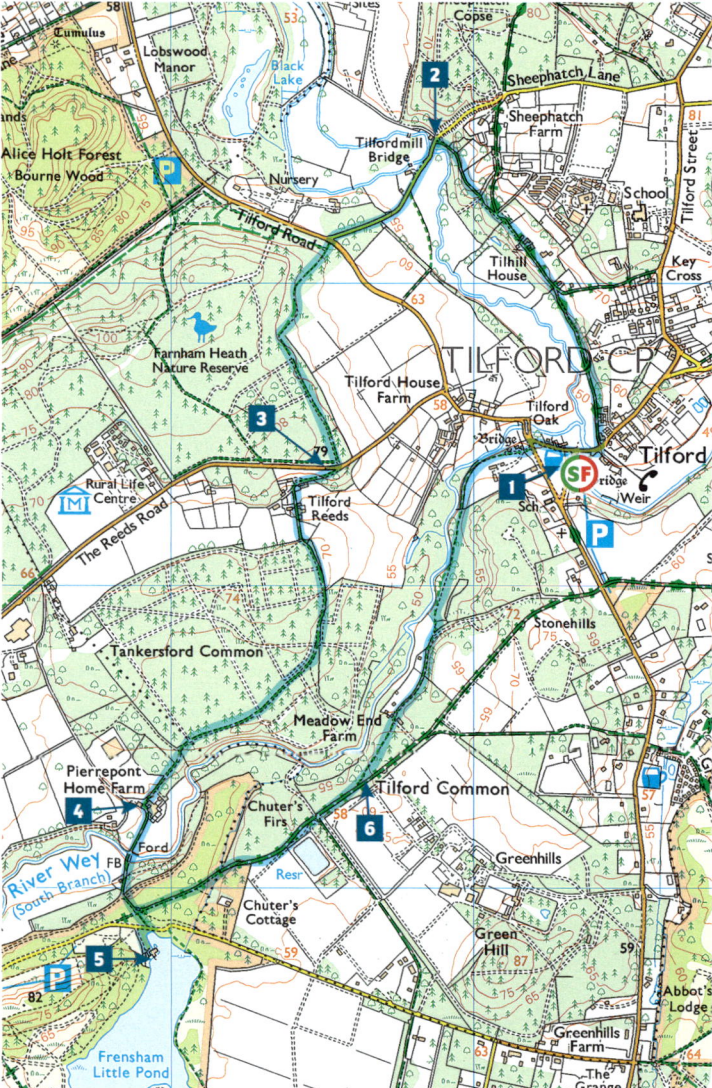

Tankerford Common

1 From the village green cross **Tilford East Bridge** and then take the footpath to the left by the pillbox. Follow this narrow path (alongside a meadow) for a few minutes and upon reaching a tarmac road, go left. Pass a farm (**Tilhill House**) and soon the road becomes a wide footpath. When it splits take the left branch through woodland. Ignoring a track joining from the left, continue straight on as the path drops down.

2 Reach a road (**Sheephatch Lane**), go left to cross over Tilfordmill Bridge and continue along the lane. At the junction cross Tilford Road and enter **Farnham Heath Nature Reserve**. Notice a lime kiln on the right-hand side of the path. There is a network of footpaths in the woodland – follow the wide well-trodden path straight on, ignoring any paths joining from the right. Walk alongside a fence and reach a road about 10–15min after entering the woodland.

3 Cross the road and continue along a track towards farm buildings. Follow the public bridleway, passing some buildings and then the path runs between fences. Stay on the bridleway through the heathland of **Tankersford Common** to reach **Pierrepont Farm**, which sells cheese and craft beer.

4 Skirt around the farm buildings, ignoring a road on the right, and then continue on a path. Shortly afterwards cross the wooden footbridge over the **River Wey South Branch**. Ignore a path on the right and continue straight

Footbridge near Pierrepont Farm

on and a few minutes beyond the bridge reach a track. Go left and then immediately right on a path. When the path splits keep right and follow it through shrubs to a road. Cross the road and head towards the cafe building and **Frensham Little Pond**.

5 The bank of the pond is an ideal place for a picnic. From the pond return to the track and turn right. Shortly after cross a wooden bridge over a stream(bed) and follow the broad track for about 10min.

6 Leave the track to the left through a kissing gate and follow the footpath past a farm building and continue along a track. Leave this track to the left on a path and walk alongside a fence and soon by the river. This path takes you back to **Tilford** village green.

It is believed that the ford at Tilford was created by the monks of Waverley Abbey in 1128 and the bridge was constructed in 1286. The recently restored medieval bridge connects Rushmoor and Tilford.

+ To lengthen

Follow the path around Frensham Little Pond, adding 2.5km (about 1hr) to the walk.

Fernsham Little Pond is a perfect place for a picnic

Frensham Little Pond

Frensham Little Pond was created in the 13th century when William de Raleigh, Bishop of Winchester, ordered ponds to be created at Frensham to supply fresh fish for his visits to Farnham Castle. The pond was drained during WW2 to prevent it being used as a landmark by the enemy, and the area was used as a tank training ground. After the war it was cleared of shrubs, the 13th-century dam was repaired and the pond re-filled. Today it is a sanctuary for wildlife.

WW2 history on the Moore Park Heritage Trail

WALK 2

Crooksbury Hill and Waverley Abbey

Time: 2hr
Distance: 6.5km (3¾ miles)
Climb: 145m

Romantic abbey ruins and a climb through woodlands to Crooksbury Hill

Start/finish	*Waverley Abbey House gate on B3001*
Locate	*GU9 8EP ///serves.duet.collected*
Cafes/pubs	*Cafes, pubs and restaurants in Farnham, none along the trail*
Transport	*Take Waverley Lane (B3001) from Farnham. Bus from Farnham*
Parking	*Small car park at the bend in the road*
Toilets	*No public toilets available*

The route starts and finishes near Waverley Abbey, a short walk from the small parking area. Make sure you allow some extra time to explore the impressive 13th-century ruins before or after the walk. The route described here follows a section of the North Downs Way (NDW) through woodland and then climbs Crooksbury Hill from where you can enjoy the views.

Stone bridge by the ruins of Waverley Abbey

1 From the car park go right and follow **Waverley Lane**, crossing over the river. At the road junction continue towards Guildford. Almost immediately leave the road to the left on a public footpath through the driveway of Stella Lodge. Follow the narrow path alongside a fence, then soon go through a kissing gate.

2 Pass **Mother Ludlam's Cave**. Follow the Heritage Trail through **Moor Park**, passing a pill box and information board about the area during WW2.

Join a sealed road near a house and soon pass by the main buildings of the estate.

According to legend, the Devil in disguise asked to borrow a cauldron from Mother Ludlam, the witch who lived in the cave. When she refused, the Devil stole the cauldron, but as he leaped away he dropped it. Mother Ludlam recovered it and placed it in Frensham Church for safe-keeping.

Mother Ludlam's Cave

3 Just before you reach the gate, turn right on the narrow NDW path. Shortly after reach a tarmac road and turn right. After 80m leave this tarmac road to the left on a narrow path. Follow the NDW signs through a kissing gate and alongside grazing land. Upon reaching the Runfold Wood information board continue straight on along the NDW. Shortly after, at a junction with signpost follow the NDW to the right through woodland.

4 At the next junction where the NDW goes left, carry straight on along a public bridleway. Walk through woodland, with a fence on your left. Ignore a path on the right and shortly after emerge onto a tarmac road. Keep right (ignoring Campton Road) and follow Crooksbury Road for about 150m.

> ℹ️ *Starting from Farnham, the North Downs Way long-distance trail traverses the Surrey Hills and continues through the Kent Downs to Dover.*

5 Turn left on Botany Hill Road and follow it for about 400m.

6 Go right on the public bridleway and when it splits keep right through woodland. At the junction – joining the signposted Spider Trail – keep

Excellent views from the top of Crooksbury Hill.

left. Follow the Spider Trail signs uphill through woodland, keeping right at the next three junctions to reach **Crooksbury Hill** and enjoy the views.

7 From the top follow the steep steps downhill with the hilltop marker behind you. Reach a car park after a few minutes, then walk to the road and turn left. Follow this narrow tarmac road for a few minutes. Take extra care!

8 Turn right by Waverley Cottage along a public bridleway. Pass some cottages to reach **Waverley Lane**. Turn right and follow the lane back to the start.

− To shorten

From Crooksbury Road at (Waypoint 5) turn right on Camp Hill Road, which takes you back to Stella Lodge saving 2km (30–40min).

Waverley Abbey

The ruins of Waverley Abbey

Waverley Abbey was the first Cistercian monastery in Britain, founded in 1128 when a small group of monks from France settled by the River Wey. The buildings were badly damaged by flood in 1201 and the abbey was rebuilt during the 13th century. The monks farmed the land and were active in the wool trade and also provided shelter for pilgrims and travellers. In 1536, as part of Henry VIII's Dissolution of the Monasteries, the abbey was suppressed and then largely demolished. The impressive remains include the fine 13th-century vaulted refectory (dining hall).

Highland cattle grazing in Highcombe Bottom

WALK 3
Devil's Punch Bowl

Time: 2½hr
Distance: 8km (5 miles)
Climb: 195m

Hidden history and some surprising views

Start/finish	*Devil's Punch Bowl, Hindhead*
Locate	*GU26 6AG ///swordfish.producing.cinemas*
Cafes/pubs	*Cafe at National Trust car park, pub and cafes in Hindhead*
Transport	*Take A3 to Hindhead. Buses from Haslemere*
Parking	*National Trust car park. Alternative parking in Hindhead, or in Highcombe Edge car park*
Toilets	*At start*

According to legend, the Devil tormented Thor, the god of thunder, by jumping from hill to hill. Thor tried to strike the Devil with lightning and once he scooped up a handful of earth and threw it at him. The depression he made is the Devil's Punch Bowl. A signposted trail follows the rim of the depression and then drops down to the bottom before climbing to Gibbet Hill.

Views over the Devil's Punch Bowl

1 From the National Trust cafe pass some picnic benches and head to the Devil's Punch Bowl viewpoint. The bowl shape is obvious from here, and you can peek down to the depression. Look for the purple arrow with 'Roam 639' on the left, which this trail follows. Leaving the picnic area

behind, ignore any side paths and follow the track through woodland for about 10min and reach Highcombe Edge car park.

2 Go through the gate and walk across the open area. When the path splits by the heathland information

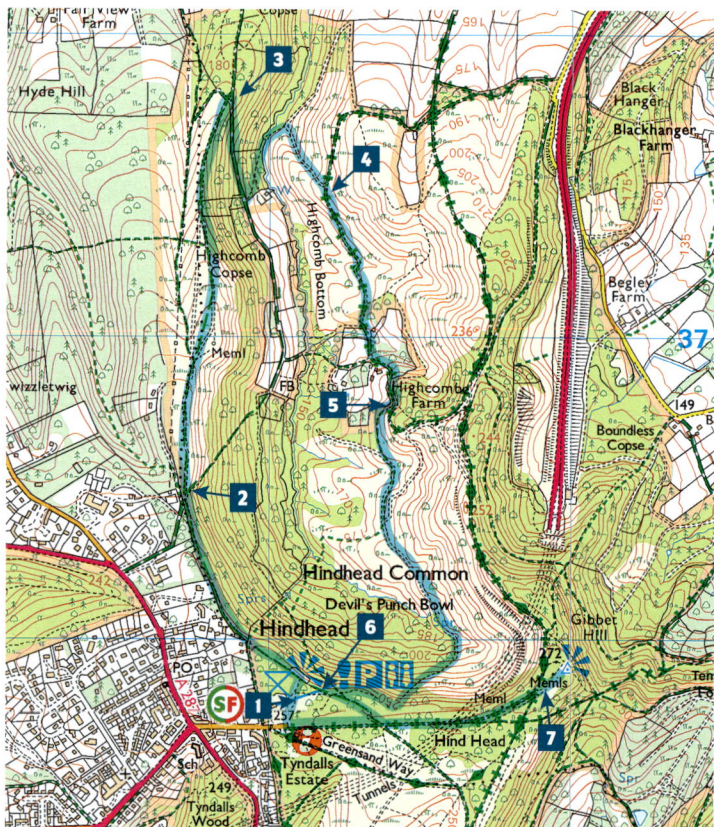

Gibbet Hill

board take the right branch with some views of the bowl. A little way on keep right on the narrow path that runs parallel to the main path and takes you to the **Robertson Memorial** and viewpoint. Shortly after, rejoin the main path and go right.

3 Turn sharply right at the junction with trail signs. The well-trodden track then drops down. A few minutes later reach the bottom and keep left towards a cottage. Carry straight on to return direct to the car park. Cross the stream over a small wooden bridge, go through the gate and turn right uphill.

4 When you reach a track go right, and then ignoring a path on the left go through a gate. Pass Gnome Cottage. At the junction go left towards Gibbet Hill.

5 Leave the surfaced track to the right on the Roam 639 path. Go through a gate and follow the Roam 639 trail, ignoring any joining paths. At the junction take the middle path and continue uphill. Ignoring a path on the right, climb the trail's steepest section.

6 Ignore a path joining from the right and go through a kissing gate, and before you reach the car park turn left on the Roam 639 path. To shorten the walk you can return direct to the car park from here. Cross a wide track and on reaching a surfaced path go left. Pass the Sailor's Stone memorial.

7 Leave this surfaced path to the right on the Roam 639 trail and go through a gate. Walk to the trig point that marks **Gibbet Hill** and enjoy some fine views – on a clear day you can see as far as London. From Gibbet Hill retrace your steps to the paved path and follow it to back the National Trust car park.

Until the opening of the Hindhead Tunnel in 2011, the A3 ran along the rim of the Devil's Punch Bowl. The old road was buried with the soil shifted while creating the tunnel and 200,000 trees and shrubs were planted as part of the National Trust restoration project.

➖ To shorten

At the bottom of the bowl just before you turn left towards the cottage (Waypoint 3), continue straight on along the waymarked Highcombe Hike towards the cafe saving 3km (1hr).

➕ To lengthen

Carry on along the signposted Roam 639 trail which continues downhill from Gibbet Hill, passing the former site of the Temple of the Four Winds, another excellent viewpoint, before returning to the car park. It will add an extra 3km (45min) to your walk.

The Sailor's Stone

Celtic Cross on Gibbet Hill

In 1786 a sailor who was walking from London to the docks in Portsmouth was brutally murdered by three men he befriended in the pub in Thursley. The three men were tried and hanged on Gibbet Hill. A stone was erected to mark the spot where the sailor was murdered. To ease the fears and superstitions that had arisen after hanging the men, in 1851 Sir William Erle, a lawyer and judge, paid for a Celtic Cross to be erected on Gibbet Hill.

WALK 4
Guildford and the River Wey

Time: 2hr
Distance: 7km
(4¼ miles)
Climb: 85m

A lovely river stroll and a chance to explore the historic town centre

Start/finish	*Town Bridge, Guildford*
Locate	*GU2 4HJ ///melt.firms.leader*
Cafes/pubs	*Pubs, cafes and restaurants in Guildford*
Transport	*Trains and buses to Guildford*
Parking	*Millmead car park*
Toilets	*Shalford Park, Guildford*

Just a short stroll from Guildford town centre you will find yourself on a stunning riverside path. Follow the snaking River Wey, watch the narrowboats navigating through locks and enjoy the views from St Catherine's Hill. Return to Guildford and allow some time to explore the town centre and visit one of the old pubs.

The River Wey by the Millmead Lock in Guildford

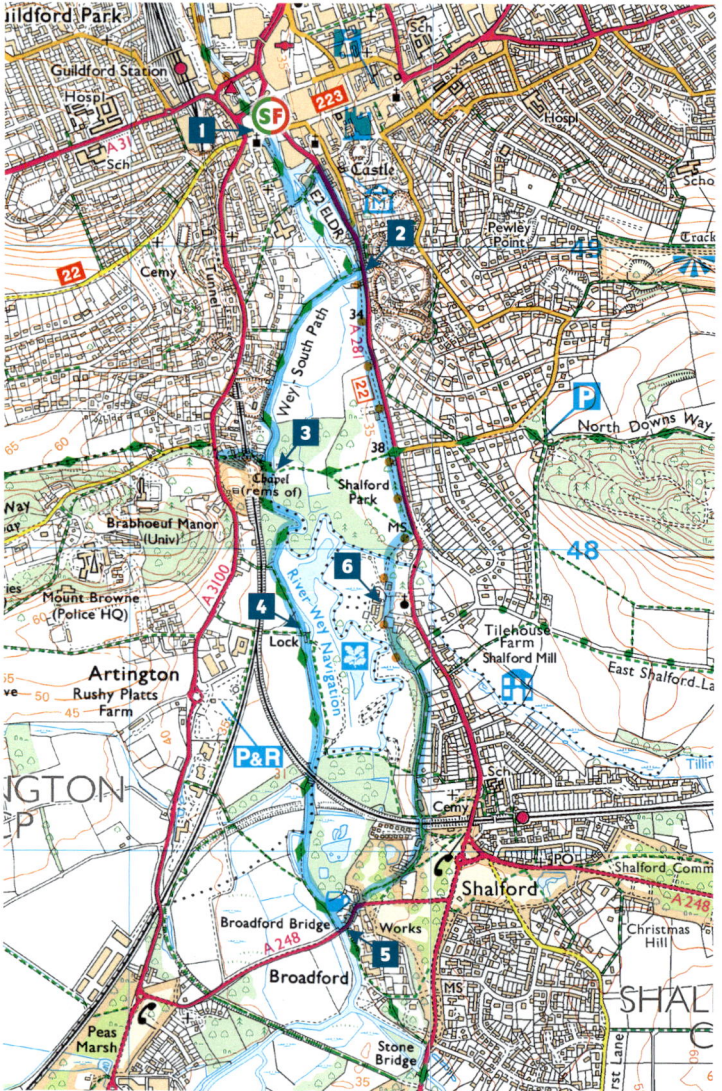

White House pub, St Nicolas's church and Town Bridge, Guildford

1 From **Town Bridge** take Millmead Road between the White Horse pub and St Nicolas's church. Look out for the sculpture of Alice and the White Rabbit on the grass. Cross the footbridge at the end of the car park, and cross over another footbridge by Millmead Lock. Reach Millbrook Road (**A281**) and turn right.

The first wooden bridge built in AD920 alongside a ford was replaced by a stone bridge in 1200, which was then adapted when the river navigation was created in 1760. After it was badly damaged by a flood in 1900 the bridge was rebuilt as a single-span iron bridge.

ⓘ *Lewis Caroll (1832–1898) – author of* Alice's Adventures in Wonderland *– spent some time in Guildford and there are sculptures of some of the characters from his books dotted around town.*

2 Just after the Weyside pub go right over the footbridge and join the tow-path. Follow the snaking path with the **River Wey** on your left.

3 Where a stream joins the River Wey, go right to make a short detour to St Catherine's Hill. Ascend the narrow road passing cottages and then take the path uphill on the left

St Catherine's Chapel

(before reaching the road). Climb to the ruins of the 14th-century **chapel** and enjoy the splendid view. From St Catherine's Hill return to the towpath and continue by the river, passing a footbridge.

4 Follow the path alongside the river and shortly pass **St Catherine's Lock**. The path then goes beneath a rail bridge. Notice the pillbox on your right just after the rail bridge.

5 When you reach a road bridge carrying the A428, go left over the bridge and pass some houses. Leave the pavement to the left on a footpath, marked as 'Bike Route 22' towards Guildford. Ignore other paths, and passing some cottages follow the bike route over a rail bridge and through some woods. In the bend of the paved path continue slightly left past a gate downhill.

6 Emerge from the woodland, passing a waterworks building and follow the bike path straight on. Soon skirt around **Shalford Park** to come out on the road near the Weyside pub and from there retrace your steps to the start.

– To shorten

Returning to the river from St Catherine's Hill, take the first footbridge. Take the path across Shalford Park towards to A281, go left and follow the bike path back to the town centre saving 4km (1hr).

+ To lengthen

If you want to enjoy the Riverside Walk further, follow the towpath all the way to Godalming (7km from Town Bridge). From Godalming you can catch a train back to Guildford.

River Wey Navigation

River Wey Navigation

The River Wey was made navigable in 1653 when the River Wey Navigation opened, with 12 locks between Weybridge and Guildford. The Godalming Navigation, with a further four locks, was completed in 1754. It was used for transporting goods for over 300 years and some commercial traffic remained until the early 1980s. Since 1964 it has been managed by the National Trust.

A section of narrow path on the Downs Link

WALK 5

St Martha's Hill and Chilworth Gunpowder Mills

Time: 3hr
Distance: 8km (5 miles)
Climb: 225m

A walk along the North Downs Way, with a short climb to St Martha's Hill and a descent to an old gunpowder mill

Start/finish	Chantry Wood car park, Guildford
Locate	GU4 8AW ///relate.forum.boxer
Cafes/pubs	Pub in Chilworth (short detour)
Transport	From A281 take Pilgrims Way. Trains to Guildford station 2km from start
Parking	Chantries car park or Halfpenny Lane car park (for shorter walk)
Toilets	No public toilets available

Follow the North Downs Way (NDW) to St Martha's Hill and admire the views from the church before descending to the River Tillingbourne. Explore the remains of the historic gunpowder mill and return via Chantry Wood. The woodland is spectacular in the spring when it is carpeted with bluebells.

St Martha's Hill and church

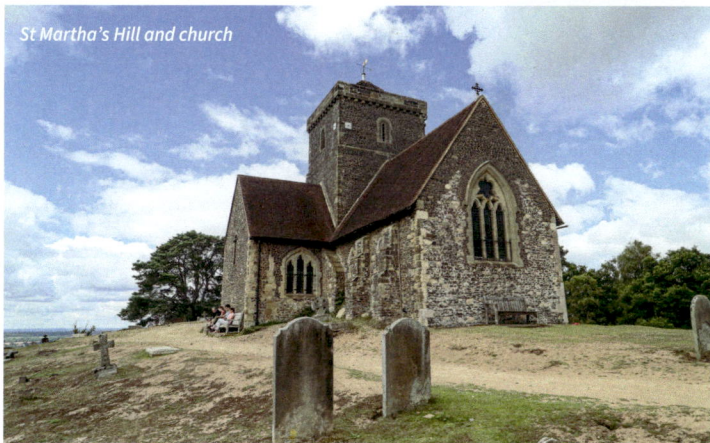

Bluebells carpet the forest floor in spring

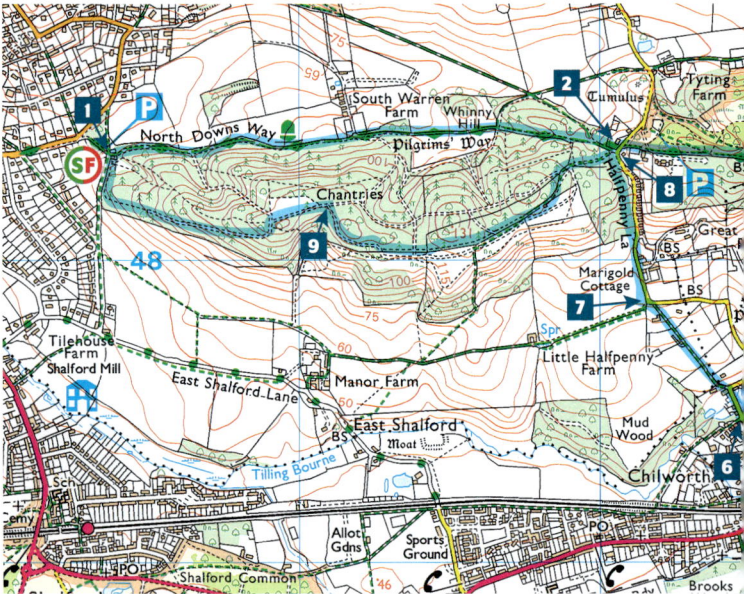

1 From the car park take the **NDW**, which follows the track along the edge of the woodland with occasional views towards Pewley Down. Pass a farm and shortly after walk alongside pastures. At the junction continue straight ahead on the NDW, ignoring any other paths.

2 Emerge onto the sealed Halfpenny Lane and turn left. A few metres later leave the road to the right by a cottage. Pass Halfpenny Lane car park on your left and continue to follow the NDW, initially through an open area and then through woodland.

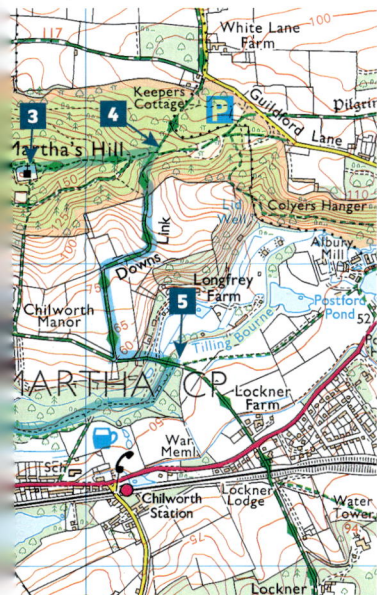

3 Reach **St Martha's Hill** and walk around the church to admire some great views of the hills. The NDW drops down on the sandy path, which splits and rejoins a few times as you descend to a junction near a WW2 pillbox.

There has been a church on St Martha's Hill since the 12th century, but after falling into ruins it was rebuilt in 1848–50. It is the only church in Surrey that is located on the Pilgrims Way and is accessible only by foot.

4 Go sharply right on the **Downs Link**, which descends through woodland. Then follow the narrow path alongside a field and keep left (ignoring a path on the right going uphill). At the junction with a signpost join a track follow the Downs Link to the left. Pass a farm and cross the **River Tillingbourne**.

5 Take the second path on the right, go through a barrier and past an information board. Follow the Chilworth Gunpowder Mills Heritage Trail, passing some mill buildings and shortly afterwards a picnic site. Follow the well-trodden path past some ruins and a row of millstones. Continue straight on, ignoring other paths, and soon go through a gate by a building.

Joining the Downs Link for a short section

6 Emerge onto Blacksmiths Lane and turn right. Pass Powdermills Fishery and some houses and at the sharp right bend of the lane go left on a path alongside a fence. Follow the narrow path alongside a field for a few minutes and reach a tarmac road (**Halfpenny Lane**).

7 Go left and a few metres later take the footpath through a gate by the house. Keep right and walk alongside the field. Entering the woodland, the path splits – take the right path and ascend almost parallel to the road.

8 Reach a big path junction with a map board at Chantry Woods. Turn left and follow the wide path. Chantry Woods are criss-crossed with several unmarked paths. Take the wide main path and soon pass a large grassy area with fire pits and a toilet building (this used to be a campsite). Follow the forest path that runs parallel to the field with views on your left. When it splits take the well-trodden path to the left close to the fields, then turn right along the wide path by the information board.

9 As the trees thin out, reach a T-junction and turn left. Follow this obvious path, passing a bench with a great view of Guildford Cathedral. After the viewpoint the path splits – for a gentle descent take the path on the left and follow it through the forest for about 10min. At a clearing with wooden cabins on the left, turn left to arrive back at Chantry Woods car park.

– To shorten

Start and finish the walk at Halfpenny Lane car park to make a circuit of 4–4.5km (1hr 30min).

Chilworth Gunpowder Mills

Millstones along the path at the site of the gunpowder mills

Chilworth Gunpowder Mills were founded by the East India Company in 1626 to supply its forces abroad. Until the mid-19th century, when high explosives were developed, gunpowder was the only explosive available for military use and for nearly 300 years it was manufactured in the valley using the power of the River Tillingbourne.

Approaching Unstead Lock on the River Wey Navigation

WALK 6

Bramley old railway and the River Wey

Time: 2½hr
Distance: 8km (5 miles)
Climb: 75m

A gentle walk along an old railway line followed by a stunning river path

Start/finish	*Bramley and Wonersh old railway station, Bramley*
Locate	*GU5 0AZ ///riots.covers.traded*
Cafes/pubs	*Pub and cafe in Bramley, pub by the river*
Transport	*Take A281 from Guildford. Bus from Guildford*
Parking	*Car park by the old railway station*
Toilets	*No public toilets available*

This easy walk first follows a disused railway line and then heads along the towpath alongside the River Wey, where you can watch the narrowboats navigate the locks. Leaving the river path, the walk follows a section of the Fox Way trail through woodland before returning to Bramley.

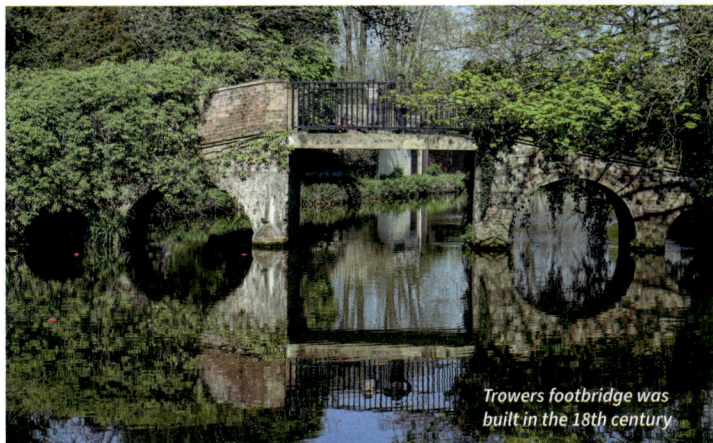

Trowers footbridge was built in the 18th century

1 From the old station walk towards Guildford and Godalming along the old railway line. Pass under the road bridge and continue along the railway past a viewing platform with picnic tables.

2 Walk over a bridge and then cross the **A281** road. Continue straight ahead along the path and a few minutes later cross the bridge over the **River Wey** and go down to the towpath. Follow the sometimes narrow towpath with the river on your left.

3 Walk on a wooden bridge and then pass **Unstead Lock**. Cross a minor road and continue on the towpath alongside the river. Look out for a WW2 pillbox on your right. Ignore any paths on the right and stay by the river. Pass some cottages and a pub's (Beefeater) garden.

> ⓘ *Pillboxes were built as part of the defence line in the 1940s. They were located along natural obstacles such as rivers and housed a machine gun and anti-tank weapons.*

4 When you reach a narrow road go left over Trowers Bridge. Walk alongside fields, ignoring a public footpath on the left and pass Bunkers Hill Farm. Just after the farm look out for the Fox

Way sign and go left. Walk through woodland (**Unsted Wood**) with a fence on your left. At the end of fence turn left on the Fox Way slightly uphill. Notice some old mighty chestnut trees in the woodland. Soon you walk alongside a fence with views towards the Hogs Back and Woking in the distance. Ignore a public footpath on the right and descend alongside the fence. The path becomes a track by a cottage.

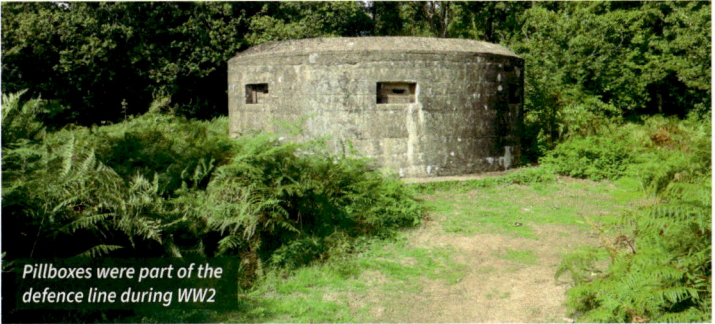

Pillboxes were part of the defence line during WW2

5 Passing some cottages cross Foxborrow Hill Road and continue on a path alongside **Bramley Golf Course**, ignoring any paths on the right. After a short descent arrive at a track (Clock House Lane) and carry straight on.

6 At the A281 road turn right. A couple of minutes later turn left by the petrol station onto Station Road, which leads in a few minutes back to **Bramley** and the start.

> **+ To lengthen**
>
> Stay on the towpath alongside the River Wey and follow it to Godalming (2km), then return to Trowers Bridge (Waypoint 4) to continue the walk.

Bramley and Wonersh station

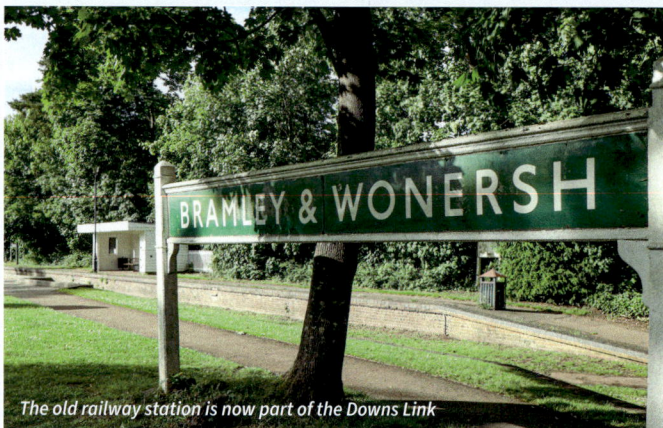

The old railway station is now part of the Downs Link

Bramley railway station opened in 1865 on the Cranleigh line, which linked Guildford, on the London–Portsmouth line, and Horsham. The station was known as Bramley and Wonersh from 1888. The line closed in 1965 and the station building was demolished a few years later. The trackbed was left to overgrow and was only brought back in use as a footpath in the 1980s. Today it is part of the Downs Link, a popular public footpath that connects the North Downs Way with the South Downs Way.

WALK 7
Newlands Corner and Silent Pool

Time: 2½hr
Distance: 8km
(5 miles)
Climb: 185m

Stroll through woods and fields with some of the best views in Surrey

Start/finish	*Newlands Corner*
Locate	*GU4 8SE ///nobody.leads.detail*
Cafes/pubs	*Cafe at Newlands Corner, refreshments at Silent Pool*
Transport	*Take A25. Bus from Guildford*
Parking	*Plenty of parking in Newlands Corner car park*
Toilets	*At start*

Follow a section of the North Downs Way (NDW) through woodland and then drop down to the mysterious Silent Pool where you can treat yourself with some local gin. Then walk alongside fields with views towards the ridge line before climbing back to Newlands Corner. The walk described here mainly follows the signposted Deer Trail.

Open fields allow for views of the North Downs

1 From the car park join the North Downs Way and head towards the A25 (**Sheer Road**). Cross the A25 and follow the NDW through woodland along a wide path (can be muddy in places in winter). Pass a viewpoint with a sculpture on the right-hand side. Follow this well-trodden path – marked as 'Deer Trail' – for about 2km, ignoring the other paths on the right.

2 At a path junction with a wooden signpost turn right downhill alongside a fence, leaving the NDW. The path descends steeply through woodland.

Pass a pillbox on the left but ignore any paths on the left. Walk alongside Albury Vineyard and just before you reach the vineyard buildings, take the path on the left leading down on steps to **Silent Pool**.

3 From Silent Pool go right on the wide path with **Sherbourne Pond** on your left. Pass the vineyard entrance and head towards the road. Carefully cross the **A25** and go left on the other side. At the junction go right and follow the footpath on the left-hand side of the road.

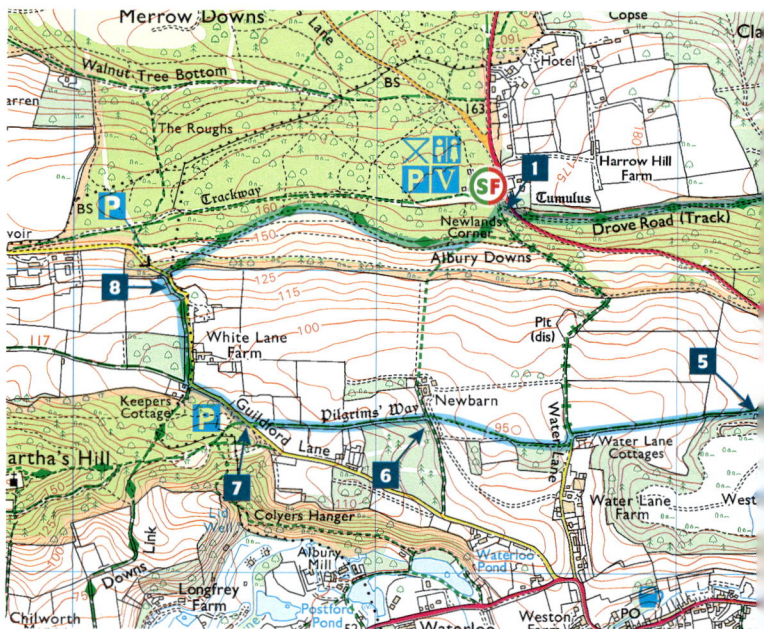

Steep descent to Silent Pool

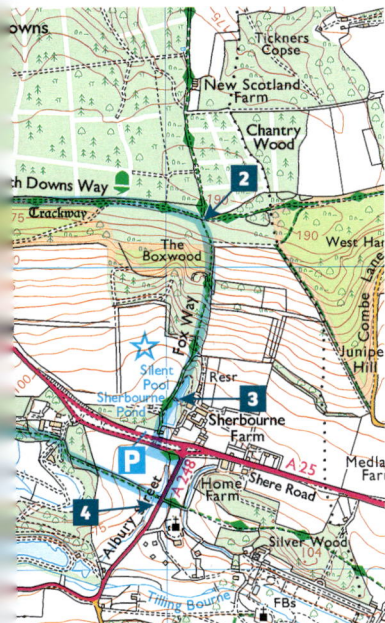

> (i) **The woodlands of Surrey supplied wood that was widely used for timber-framed buildings in the 14th and 15th centuries.**

4 Just before a church turn right and cross the road. Go through a kissing gate, cross the stream and walk across a field. At the end of the field clamber over the stile and continue through woodland. A few minutes later pass the gate of the **Sand Pit** and continue straight on.

5 Join a track, keep left and shortly after pass a cottage and then walk alongside fields with views of the North Downs ridge. The path becomes a track by a group of cottages. Descend to a junction, cross

Magnificent views of the hills from a section of the Pilgrims' Way

the track (Water Lane) and the Deer Trail continues on its other side slightly to the left. Ascend through the woods and soon the views open up towards fields and meadows.

6 At the path junction with a signpost near a farm (**Newbarn**) continue straight on. To shorten your walk go right here to return to Newlands Corner.

7 A few minutes later emerge onto **Guildford Lane** and turn right. Follow the road past a car park to reach **Keepers Cottage**. Go through the gate and turn right on the NDW footpath that runs parallel to the road.

> (i) *The Surrey Hills was one of the first areas in the country to become an AONB in 1958.*

8 When you reach the tarmac road again, cross it and climb through woodland. Follow the NDW signs and at the junction go right, then keep on the upper path on the grassy hillside. Stay on the NDW a little longer for more views of St Martha's Hill and the fields below. Climb the hillside with benches to reach **Newlands Corner** and the car park.

▬ To shorten

At the path junction near Newbarn Farm, go right to return to Newlands Corner saving 2km (30min).

✚ To lengthen

From Guildford Lane continue on the Deer Trail that takes you up to St Martha's Hill and then rejoins the described trail near Keepers Cottage. Allow an extra 40–45min.

Silent Pool

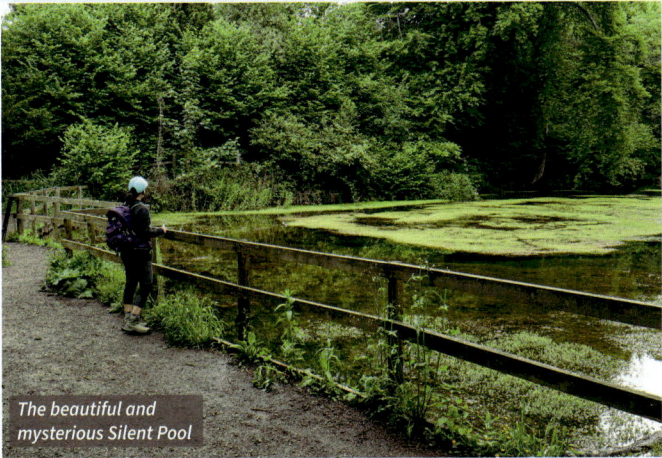

The beautiful and mysterious Silent Pool

An eerie stillness lingers above Silent Pool. Legend tells of the fate of a wood-cutter's daughter who bathed in the pool. She was surprised by a nobleman who tried to lure her to the bank but she moved to the deeper water where she drowned. When the woodcutter returned he found her body and the nobleman's hat floating in the water. The hat bore the crest of Prince John. Today it is an ideal place to stop for a picnic or visit the Silent Pool Distillery located next to the pond.

Gentle descent to Gomshall

WALK 8
Shere woodlands

Time: 1¾hr
Distance: 5km (3 miles)
Climb: 150m

Start/finish	*Middle Street, Shere*
Locate	*GU5 9HF ///flags.daisy.retain*
Cafes/pubs	*Cafes and pubs in Shere*
Transport	*Take A25 to Shere. Train to Gomshall station, bus from Guildford*
Parking	*Shere village car park*
Toilets	*In old fire station, Shere*

A woodland walk and a picturesque village with pleasant pubs

This leafy woodland walk starts and ends in the charming village of Shere where some scenes of *Bridget Jones: The Edge of Reason* and *The Holiday* were filmed. Stroll amongst old village houses and visit one of the pubs or the tea room to soak up the atmosphere.

There is dense vegetation along most of the walk

1 Start at the bridge over the **River Tillingbourne** and walk past the old fire station (now a public toilet). Follow this road and turn left at the junction. Almost immediately turn right to the village car park.

2 With the car park entrance on your right take the path through a gate. When the path splits take the right branch through woodland and cross under the A25. Just after the underpass go left uphill and then right by the **Netley Plantation** sign. Follow the path, passing a pillbox and then alongside a fence.

Old fire station building in Shere

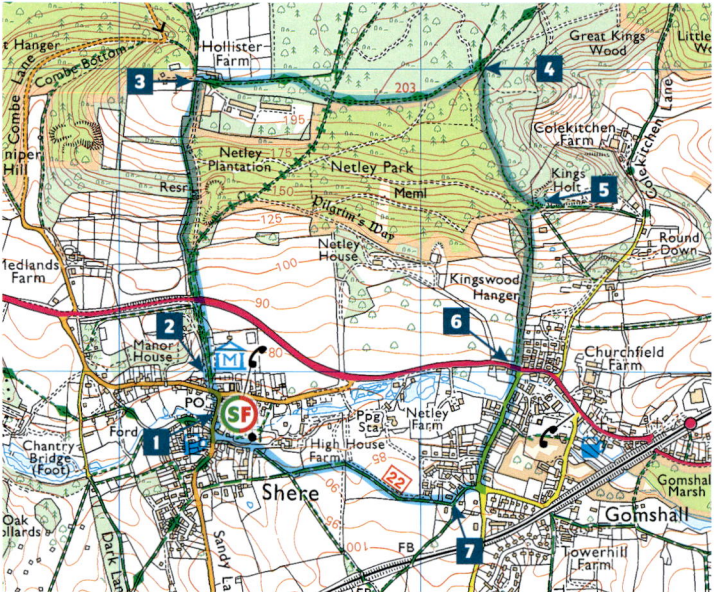

Entering Netley Plantation

> ⓘ *More than a fifth of the land area of Surrey is covered by woodland, making it England's most wooded county. A quarter of these woodlands are ancient woodlands.*

3 Reach a track by the Shere and Woodlands information board near **Hollister Farm**. Go right, passing some cottages and stables. Go through a gate and follow the well-trodden North Downs Way (NDW) for about 15min, continuing straight on at the junction. Ignore a path on the right with a National Trust Netley Park sign and continue along the edge of the parkland.

4 Leave the NDW on a public footpath at the junction with a wooden signpost. Descend on the wide path through woodland. Ignore a path marked with a yellow arrow on the right and continue straight on. Shortly afterwards, pass an overgrown pillbox on the right.

5 Take the first path on the right after the pillbox and a few metres later when the path splits go left downhill on the public footpath. At a fence and a building on your left a few metres later keep left again and descend through woodland. There is a network of paths here – stick to the most prominent path with a fence on your left.

The walk joins the North Downs Way for a short section

6 Emerge from the woodland onto **Shere Road**. Keep left and then immediately right on Queen Street. For Gomshall train station follow Shere Road past the petrol station for about 700m. Follow Queen Street by the River Tillingbourne. Pass some houses and when the pavement ends, walk on the road and then turn right on Gravel Pits Lane.

7 By Gravel Pits Farmhouse turn right along the Shere Parish Millennium Trail. Leaving the houses behind walk alongside fields for about 10min (ignoring any tracks). At the path junction go right on the Millennium Trail and shortly afterwards reach the 12th-century St James's church. Passing the church and graveyard reach the charming centre of **Shere**. Keep right just before the White Horse pub and arrive back at the start.

> **+ To lengthen**
>
> From the start follow the Fox Way past Silent Pool then turn right to join the North Downs Way. Rejoin the walk at Hollister Farm (Waypoint 3) to make an 8km circular walk.

Netley Park

Overgrown pillbox in Netley Park

Built in the late 18th century, Netley House has been through several changes over the decades. It served as a hospital during WW1 and was used by the Canadian army during WW2. The building itself is closed but Netley Park, which was created on the turn of the 19th century, is open to the public. In the woodland you can still find six of the pillboxes built on the North Downs behind Netley House during WW2.

Walking between fields near Coverwood farm

WALK 9
Hurtwood and Holmbury Hill

Start/finish	Hurtwood Inn, Peaslake
Locate	KT24 5TA ///rider.ready.jobs
Cafes/pubs	Pub in Peaslake
Transport	Leave A25 towards Gomshall. Bus from Guildford
Parking	Pond Lane car park, Peaslake
Toilets	No public toilets available

Time: 2½hr
Distance: 8km (5 miles)
Climb: 235m

A pleasant walk on tracks and paths with some of the best views of the Surrey Hills

This walk follows a section of the Greensand Way through fields and woodland to Holmbury Hill. From the hilltop you can spot nearby Leith Hill and enjoy the panoramic views. Hurt Wood is criss-crossed by miles of tracks and paths that are popular with mountain bikers as well as walkers.

The Greensand Way is well waymarked

1 With the Hurtwood Inn on your right, go left uphill just after the bike shop. Follow the paved road, passing St Mark's Church on your right through woods. Reach the cemetery and skirt around it and then follow the wide path through **Hurt Wood**. At the Y-junction with a big pile of rocks in the middle take the wide path on the left and follow it straight on for about 15min, ignoring any unmarked paths and tracks on either side.

2 Leave this path to the left on the Greensand Way (GW) by a wooden waymarker. (From here you will be following the GW signs to Holmbury Hill). Descend through woods,

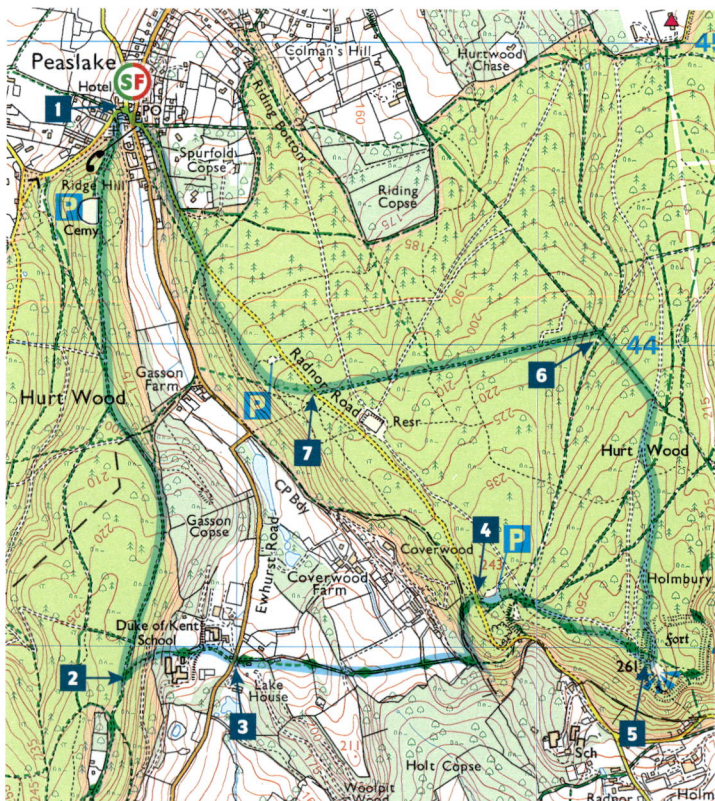

Crossing the grounds of the Duke of Kent School

crossing another path and entering the property of the **Duke of Kent School**. Follow the GW signs through the grounds to reach a narrow tarmac road by the school entrance.

> (i) *The Greensand Way traverses the ridge of greensand rocks through Surrey and Kent. It runs roughly parallel and south of the North Downs ridge.*

3 Cross the road and follow the GW squeezed between fences. After a stile the path runs alongside fields. Go through a gate near a farm and shortly after reach the woods. The path splits by a gate – go left following the GW slightly uphill, bending right to reach a tarmac road.

4 Cross the road into Hurtwood car park 1, then take the GW path to the right. Shortly after cross a wide path and continue straight on, passing a viewpoint. There is a network of paths there, but at the next three junctions keep right following the GW signs to reach **Holmbury Hill** about 15min from the car park.

5 Leave Holmbury Hill with the donation box on your left along the forest track. This section is not waymarked. Follow the forest track straight on, crossing two other tracks until it ends at a third forest track, where you turn right. Ignore paths on left and right and shortly after, at the junction where a path crosses the track, leave the track to the left on the wide path. Follow this straight on and arrive at a big track junction.

The walk can be extended to Pitch Hill

6 Take the second track from the left uphill by the Nature Reserve sign. Carry straight on for about 15–20min until you reach a narrow tarmac road, **Radnor Road**.

7 Cross the road and then keep right, following a wider path roughly parallel to the road. In about 10min reach the tarmac road again. Turn left and follow it back to **Peaslake**, opposite the Hurtwood Inn.

– To shorten

Park in Hurtwood car park 1 (Waypoint 4) and walk to Holmbury Hill and back (3km).

+ To lengthen

Before turning left to join the Greensand Way (Waypoint 3), carry on for about 500m to Pitch Hill and some fine views towards the South Downs.

Extensive views from Holmbury Hill

Holmbury Hill

Not only does it offer lovely views of nearby Leith Hill and – on a clear day – all the way to the sea, Holmbury Hill is also the site of an Iron Age fort, which was excavated in 1929. Believed to have been built between 150 and 50bc, it was defended by double ramparts to the west and north with escarpments on the eastern and southern slopes.

One of the horseshoe-shaped Lovelace bridges

WALK 10
The Lovelace Bridges

Time: 2hr
Distance: 6.5km
(4 miles)
Climb: 145m

A heritage walk through pretty woodlands

Start/finish	Green Dene, near East Horsley
Locate	KT24 5TA ///rider.ready.jobs
Cafes/pubs	Pub in East Horsley (2km off route)
Transport	From A246 take Green Dene Road. Train to Horsley station (4km from start)
Parking	Green Dene car park
Toilets	No public toilets available

The signposted Lovelace Bridges Trail takes you through woodland where you can explore a number of unusual Victorian bridges. Cross over and walk under the bridges as you follow the path through the lush woods and around fields. Take some time to admire the individually designed structures. This bridleway is popular with horse riders so can sometimes be muddy underfoot.

The walk goes through thickly forested areas

1 From Green Dene car park cross the road and take the path through the woods. A few minutes later reach a wide path and turn left. Pass Forest Lodge and turn right along the road.

2 After about 200m leave the road to the left on a marked path through a barrier. Follow signs for the Lovelace Bridge Trail, turning sharply left. At the path junction keep left and a few minutes later at the next path junction go left to make a short detour to Raven Arch. From the bridge return to the path junction and continue left. A few minutes later keep left on the marked trail.

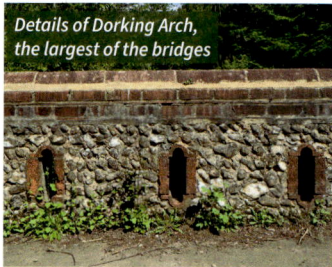

Details of Dorking Arch, the largest of the bridges

ⓘ *The Surrey Hills AONB is one of 37 nationally protected landscapes in England, and enjoys equal protection from development as a national park.*

Briary Hill East bridge

3 Cross Dorking Arch over **Crocknorth Road**. Ignore any joining paths and at the junction follow the footpath straight on. At the site of Oak Hangers Bridge go left, entering Oldlands by a sign and then keep right. Shortly afterwards, go left on the narrow bridleway. At the junction with signposts continue straight ahead on the bridleway and reach Stoney Dene Bridge.

4 Just before Stoney Dene Bridge go right downhill. Join the path running under the bridge and keep right. A few minutes later at the path junction go right and shortly after at the next intersection continue straight on. At the next path junction take the middle path along the edge of **Pump Pond Wood** and pass Horse Close Bridge. The path runs alongside a fence by a field. Chestnut, oak and some pine trees form the woodland here.

5 At the corner of the fence at the junction turn right and follow the fence line skirting around the field. Reach **Crocknorth Farm** and continue straight on, passing some stables and cottages.

6 At **Crocknorth Road** cross over to continue along the Lovelace Bridge Trail. Follow the path through woodland, passing under Briary Hill East Bridge. At the junction continue straight on and under Briary Hill West Bridge. Before long arrive at the junction where you can spot Raven Arch straight on. Turn left and retrace your steps to the car park.

— To shorten

For a 3.5km (1hr 15min) circular walk, at the site of Oak Hangers Bridge turn right and follow the path to reach a junction at Crocknorth Farm. Turn right here and follow the description from Waypoint 5.

The Lovelace Bridges

In the 1860s the owner of East Horsley Estate, Lord Lovelace, had some tracks built with gentle inclines to facilitate the transport of timber by horse-drawn carts in the hilly woods. Embankments were constructed over small valleys and some crossing tracks were bridged. There were 15 horseshoe-shaped bridges, of which ten remain, although some are on private land. Made of brick and flint, the bridges were individually designed and ornately decorated.

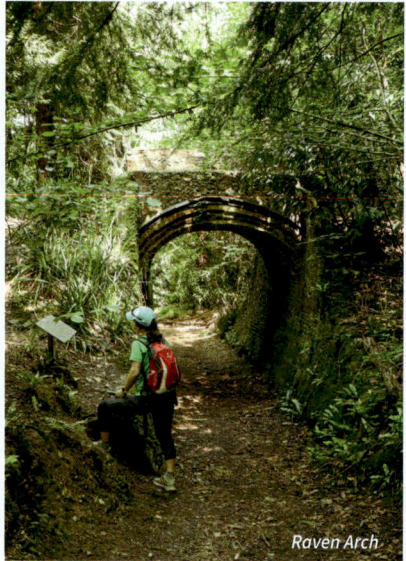

Raven Arch

WALK 11
Denbies Hillside and vineyard

Time: 2hr
Distance: 6km
(3¾ miles)
Climb: 160m

A gentle walk through vineyards with lovely views to Box Hill

Start/finish	Dorking railway station
Locate	KT24 5TA ///rider.ready.jobs
Cafes/pubs	Pubs, cafes and restaurants in Dorking, cafe and restaurant at Denbies Wine Estate
Transport	From M25 take A24. Trains from London and Guildford
Parking	Dorking Station car park. Alternative (free) car park at Denbies Wine Estate
Toilets	At station and Denbies Wine Estate

This is a gentle stroll through the biggest vineyard in England followed by a short woodland walk and a traverse on the scenic grassy chalkland of Denbies Hillside. Drink in the views of the rolling vineyards with the iconic Box Hill in the background and then sample some local wine. The vineyard is easily accessible from Dorking.

The main building of the Denbies Wine Estate

1 From the station take the underpass under the **A24** and then walk alongside it. Turn left on Ashcombe Road and follow it for about 700m.

2 Turn right on Yew Tree Road. The narrow road becomes a path and at the junction with a signpost continue straight on downhill towards Westhumble. Go through a gate and carry straight on across the vineyard. Reach a gravel path and follow it towards the **Denbies** estate buildings.

3 Near the building go left on a sealed public footpath turning away from the buildings. When the sealed path bends right, continue straight on uphill on a gravel path.

4 At the junction with a signpost go left on the North Downs Way (sealed road) through woodland. Soon views open up towards the estate and the vineyard, with Box Hill in the background. Go through two gates within 10min.

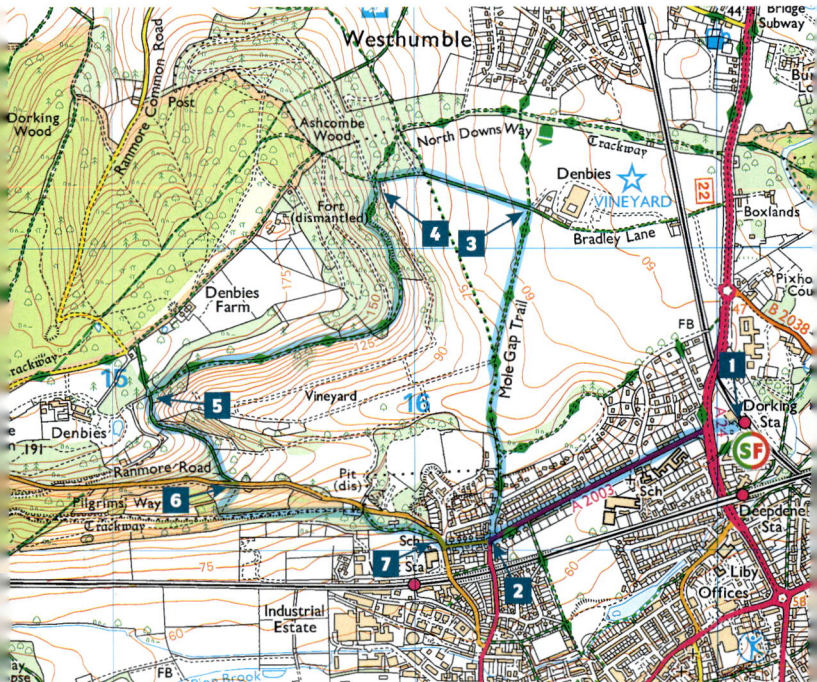

Great views of the wine estate from the hills above

The Denbies estate buildings are surrounded by rows of grapevines

> (i) **There are five vineyards producing some award-winning wines on the slopes of the chalky hills in Surrey.**

5 Reach a junction with a signpost by a gate. Leave the NDW here and follow the public bridleway to the left as it descends alongside a fence. Pass a wooden gate (you can go back to the vineyard via Leith Hill Greenway) and continue straight on downhill. At the path junction go left and reach a road.

6 Cross over the road and through a gate into Denbies Hillside area. Follow the path down the grassy hillside. Go through another gate and turn left along a wide path. Soon pass a house on your left and carry straight on, ignoring a path on the right. Walk alongside a fence and then joining another path keep right by the sealed road. Follow the path squeezed between fences.

7 On reaching a tarmac road go right and then turn left on Ashcombe Road and follow it back to the A24 and the station.

> **— To shorten**
>
> Go for a short stroll on the footpaths within the estate boundaries.
>
> **+ To lengthen**
>
> At Waypoint 4 turn right and follow the NDW to Box Hill. Return to this junction to finish the walk. This would add an extra 4km.

Entering Denbies Hillside

Denbies Wine Estate

England's largest vineyard, the Denbies Wine Estate was founded in 1984. The vineyards are situated in a protected valley of south-facing slopes on the North Downs. The grapes grown on the chalky soil in a micro-climate produce some award-winning sparkling wines. The estate welcomes visitors with a restaurant, a hotel, a shop and wine tasting tours. The paths through the vineyard provide some amazing views to the iconic Box Hill (see Walk 12).

The River Mole can be crossed on the stepping stones or on a footbridge

WALK 12
Box Hill and the Stepping Stones

Start/finish	Box Hill and Westhumble railway station
Locate	RH5 6BT ///funny.apron.storm
Cafes/pubs	Cafe at Box Hill car park
Transport	Trains from London
Parking	Box Hill Stepping Stones National Trust car park (start walk from Waypoint 5), or Box Hill National Trust car park (start walk from Waypoint 4)
Toilets	Box Hill by the cafe building

Time: 1½hr
Distance: 4.5km (2¾ miles)
Climb: 160m

A short but steep climb to the iconic Box Hill

This is a great way to explore Box Hill if you don't want to follow the longer Box Hill Hike (Walk 13). There is a short but fairly steep climb with rewarding views of Dorking town and the countryside. Take a picnic or treat yourself in the cafe before you start the descent to the River Mole.

The grassy hillside of Box Hill

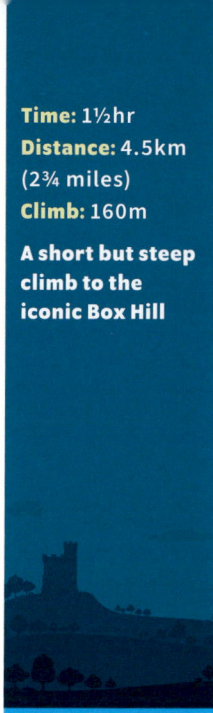

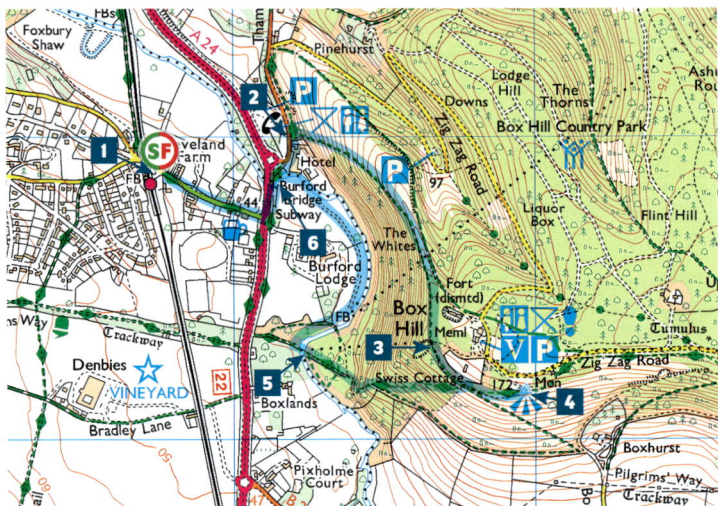

1 From the station follow Westhumble Street and take the underpass under the **A24**. Emerging on the other side keep left and pass the **Burford Bridge Hotel**.

2 Leave the pavement to the right on steps after the hotel building. Climb the waymarked Stepping Stones path, keeping right alongside a fence. Soon you have views of Dorking and the Denbies Vineyard. Ascend the chalky path, keeping close to the treeline, and when it splits keep left. Climb the grassy hillside with views of the Zig Zag Road to your left. When the path splits keep right among trees and stay on the wide chalky path, ignoring the Hill Top Stroll path on the left.

ⓘ *The chalky slopes of Box Hill are home to a variety of wild orchid species that flower between April and September. The most common is the lovely Common Spotted Orchid, but you can also spot rarer species.*

3 Pass a **memorial stone**, which marks the place where the eccentric Major Peter Labelliere was buried in June 1800. Ignore the Riverside Walk path on the left and continue through woodland. Notice some steps on the right heading down on the hillside, which you will take shortly. But first go straight through gates, keeping left to reach the Salomon's Memorial

Box Hill fort

viewpoint on **Box Hill**. Head to the National Trust cafe for refreshments and to visit the fort.

> The fort on Box Hill was built as one of 13 fortified mobilisation centres forming the defence line in the late 1800s. It was designed to gather troops and supplies and slow down French troops in the event of an invasion.

4 From the viewpoint return to the steps and go downhill through woodland on the Stepping Stones path to the **River Mole**.

5 Cross over on the stepping stones (for a footbridge option take the right fork at the junction) and follow the path with the river on your right, through woodland at first and then across the large open field of Burford Meadow.

6 Emerge onto a pavement, go left to the underpass and retrace your steps to the station.

✚ To lengthen

Choose one of the several sign-posted trails that start from the National Trust car park on Box Hill.

The stepping stones

The stepping stones were first mentioned in 1841 and were probably installed by the owner of Burford Lodge to allow access to an orchard. During WW2 the stones were removed as part of the anti-invasion measurements. They were replaced after the war and today the North Downs Way crosses the River Mole on the stepping stones.

Stepping stones across the River Mole

WALK 13
Box Hill Hike

CHALLENGE ROUTE

Time: 4hr
Distance: 12.5km (7¾ miles)
Climb: 485m

One of the more challenging routes in the Surrey Hills, with some great viewpoints along the way

Start/finish	*Box Hill National Trust car park*
Locate	*KT20 7LB ///jars.zealous.part*
Cafes/pubs	*Cafe near the car park, pub halfway around at Mickleham*
Transport	*From Mickleham take the B2209 and then Zigzag Road. No public transport*
Parking	*Box Hill car park*
Toilets	*Box Hill by the cafe building*

The signposted Box Hill Hike (BHH) might be one of the most challenging routes in the Surrey Hills. There are some steep up- and downhill sections, however your efforts will be rewarded with some great views. There are plenty of nice picnic spots or you can opt for a rest with a refreshing drink at the pub halfway around.

Broadwood's Folly on Lodge Hill

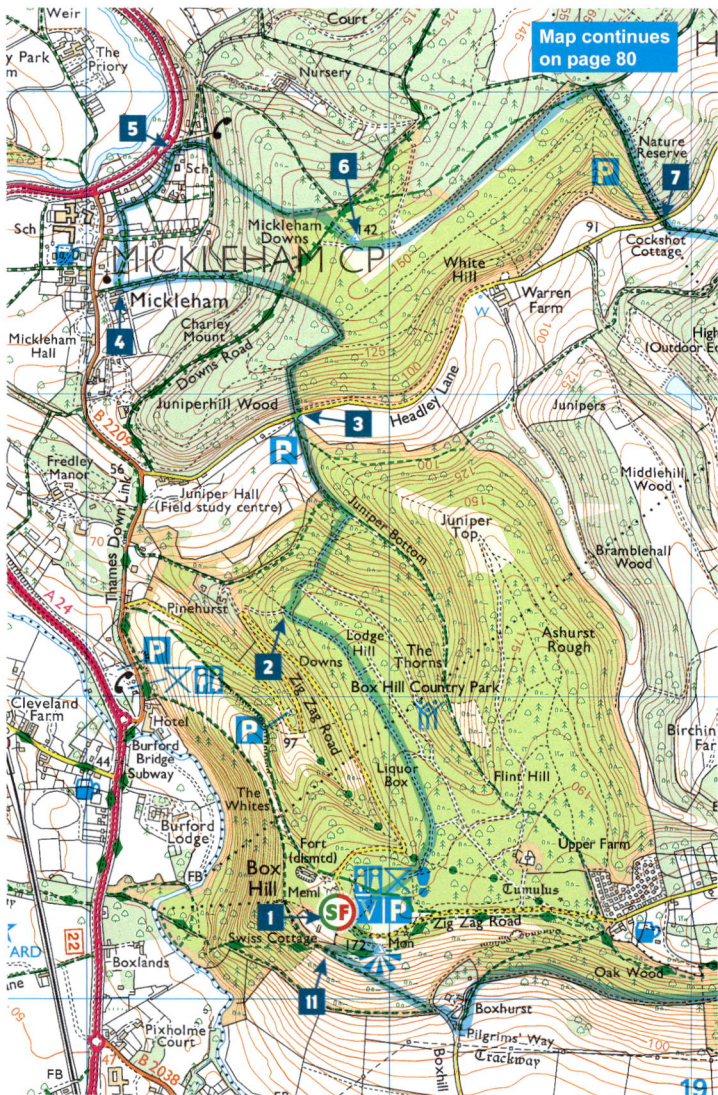

Map continues on page 80

Weir

y Park
m

The Priory

Court

Nursery

5

Sch

6

Mickleham Downs

42

7

Nature Reserve

P

91

Cockshot Cottage

Sch

MICKLEHAM C P

White Hill

Warren Farm

High (Outdoor Ed

Mickleham

Mickleham Hall

4

Charley Mount

Downs Road

Juniperhill Wood

3

Headley Lane

Junipers

B 2209

Fredley Manor

56

Thames Down Link

Juniper Hall (Field study centre)

P

Juniper Bottom

Juniper Top

Middlehill Wood

Bramblehall Wood

70

A 24

Pinehurst

Downs

2

Lodge Hill

The Thorns

Ashurst Rough

P

Cleveland Farm

Hotel

Burford Bridge Subway

44

Box Hill Country Park

Birchin Fa

P

97

Zig Zag Road

Liquor Box

Flint Hill

The Whites

Burford Lodge

FB

Box Hill

Fort (dismtd)

Meml

Upper Farm

Tumulus

1

SF

P

Swiss Cottage

17

Zig Zag Road

Oak Wood

ARD

22

Boxlands

11

Boxhurst

Pixholme Court

Pilgrims' Way Trackway

Boxhill

FB

B 2038

19

1 Locate the information board at the car park opposite the cafe and take the path marked 'BHH'. This first section of the trail is shared with other signposted trails. Follow the BHH signs through woodland and when the path splits take the left branch. Soon the views open up on your left.

2 About 20min from the car park, reach Broadwood's Tower with some views to the valley below. Keep right by the tower and descend through woodland. When the path splits follow the signs to the right. Descend on wooden steps and at the bottom of the valley go left and follow the wide path to Whitehill car park.

> Broadwood's Tower is a two-storey folly made of flint. It was built around 1815 by Thomas Broadwood, the owner of nearby Juniper Hall.

3 Cross the road and climb the steep path opposite following BHH signs. Soon there are views, then descend through woodland, ignoring a path on the right. At the next junction cross the **Thames Downs Link** path and follow BHH trail signs straight on downhill through woodland. Turn right at this junction to miss out the village. Pass a cottage and over a stile join a track heading towards a church with a graveyard in **Mickleham**.

4 At the graveyard go right through a gate. The BHH crosses the graveyard then continues alongside some cottages and gardens. Cross a road and continue on the narrow path alongside a stone wall past more gardens. At the end of the stone wall turn sharply right alongside a hedge and pass a playground and houses. On reaching a road continue straight on, passing **St Michael's School**.

5 Reach a narrow road, go right and then turn right up on the steps by the King William IV pub. After a building at the next junction continue straight on slightly uphill through woodland passing a wrecked car. At the next junction keep right and shortly after crossing another path continue straight on.

6 Emerging from the woods, follow the BHH signs slightly to the left and walk the length of The Gallops on top of **Mickleham Downs**. Pass an information board and continue through woodland, then turn right downhill just before a fence.

7 After a steep downhill section cross Headley Lane and continue on the path to the left of **Cockshot Cottage**. At the junction by **High Ashurst Outdoor Education Centre** keep right and then go left through a gate just before reaching a road. Join a track and go left downhill, ignoring any side tracks.

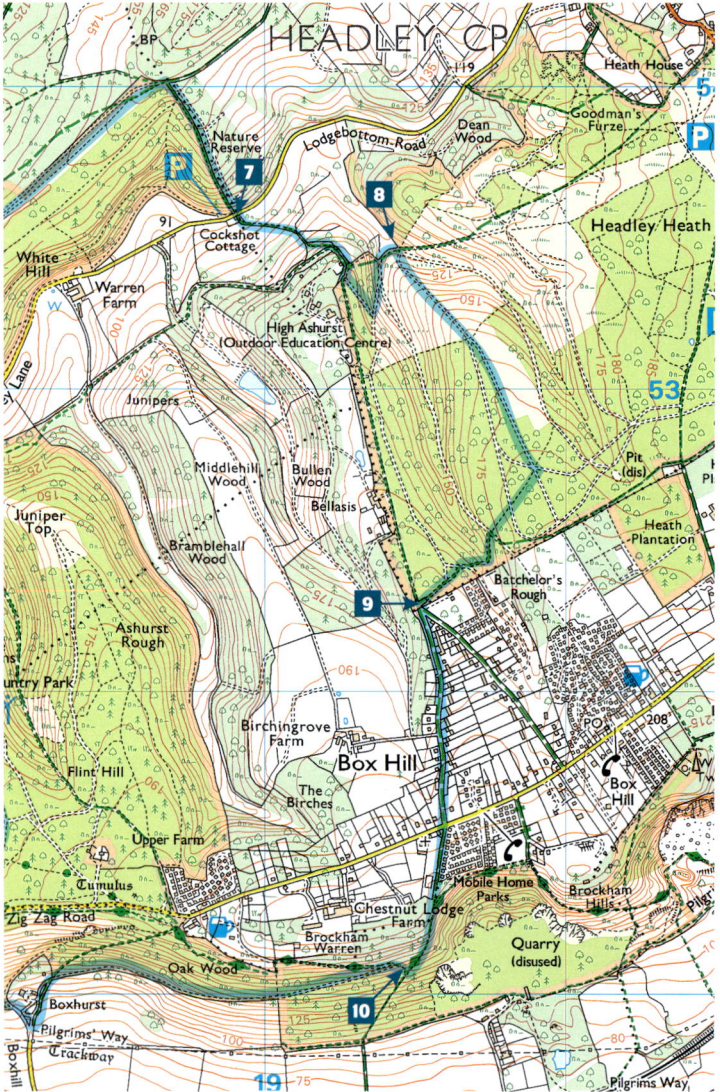

The Gallops on top of Mickleham Downs

8 Just before the track starts to climb go right uphill on steps. The path levels and at the junction follow the BHH signs to the right. At the next junction continue straight on downhill. Cross another path and continue to follow the BHH signs.

9 Go through a gate by the Headley Heath information board. Turn left and go along Headley Heath Approach in **Box Hill village**. Reach and cross a tarmac road and continue straight on by Golden Lodge, passing a mobile home park. Join the North Downs Way and carry straight on. After a short descent turn right uphill on steps.

10 At the top of the steps leave the North Downs Way and keep left. Follow the BHH with views on the left and clamber over a stile. Keep left near a gate and descend alongside a fence. At a tarmac road, keep left and a few metres later go right uphill on a path.

At a junction go left, through a kissing gate and then right uphill. Go through another gate and continue alongside a grassy hillside with some views on your left.

11 Turn sharply right by the next gate and head to **Salomon's Memorial** with some great views. From the viewpoint follow the paved path back to the car park.

— To shorten

To cut off the corner at Mickleham (saving 2km or 30min), when you reach the Thames Downs Link path (Waypoint 3) go right and right again when you next see the BHH crossing your path. Or carry straight on at the junction by the High Ashurst Outdoor Education Centre and then rejoin the trail at Waypoint 9.

Views of Dorking from the slopes of Box Hill

Box Hill

Common spotted orchid (Dactylorhiza fuchsii)

The name Box Hill refers to the ancient box woodland found on the west-facing chalk slopes. The area is habitat for 38 species of butterflies and some 17 species of orchids. The long-distance North Downs Way traverses the south-facing slope and the route of the 2012 Summer Olympics cycling road race also climbed Box Hill.

WALK 14
Leith Hill

Time: 2hr
Distance: 6km (3¾ miles)
Climb: 165m

Start/finish	Plough Inn, Coldharbour
Locate	RH5 6HD ///swear.lance.straw
Cafes/pubs	Pub in Coldharbour, refreshment kiosk at Leith Hill Tower
Transport	Take Coldharbour Lane from Dorking
Parking	Small car park in Coldharbour
Toilets	No public toilets available

Climb the highest hill in Surrey for great views

This walk takes you to the 18th-century tower on top of Leith Hill, the highest point in the Surrey Hills. On a clear day it is possible to see the English Channel to the south and buildings of London to the north. After admiring the panorama, you can visit the tower and then enjoy a pleasant woodland walk. A pub lunch in Coldharbour would round off the outing nicely.

Leith Hill is a popular picnic spot

Extensive views from the highest hilltop on the Greensand Ridge

1 Take the track opposite the Plough Inn. Pass a parking area and continue along the track past some houses. When the track splits take the right branch uphill signed 'To Tower'. Follow this until you reach the cricket ground.

2 Pass the cricket ground and continue straight ahead by the waymarkers, ignoring the path on the right. Follow the wide path through woodland, ignoring any side paths, downhill towards the tower.

3 A few minutes later at the big junction with a gully on your left take the well-trodden path steeply uphill. This part of the trail is marked with Greensand Way as well as Heathland Trail signs. After a few minutes of climbing reach **Leith Hill Tower**. Enjoy the stunning views and climb the tower (entrance fee).

> **ⓘ** *Parts of the Surrey Hills such as Box Hill and Leith Hill are owned and managed by the National Trust.*

4 Walk past the tower and take the path to the right (the other path leads to a car park). Follow this well-trodden path through woodland for a few minutes. When the path splits near a striking monkey puzzle tree, go right slightly downhill. Follow this wide path for about 15min, ignoring any side paths.

Footbridge across the River Tillingbourne

5 Reach a forest track and keep right. Shortly after, at the junction where numerous paths meet, fork right slightly uphill. Walk through woodland, ignoring any crossing paths. Reach and join a wide public footpath, keep right and follow it alongside a fence with a field on your left. When the path splits by the wooden public footpath signpost, take the right branch. Follow the well-trodden path (ignoring narrow path on the right).

6 Reach and cross a wide path by the wooden Greensand Way signpost and head towards the gate. Cross

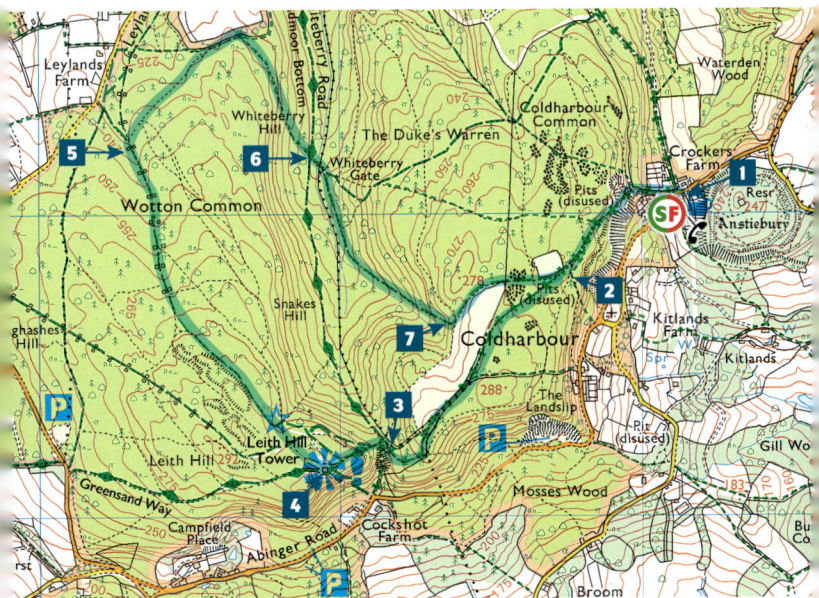

The Gothic tower on Leith Hill

Thick vegetation near Leith Hill

the River Tillingbourne over a bridge and go through the gate, entering **The Duke's Warren**. Keep right and follow the path parallel to the river until you reach another wide path by waymarkers.

7 Go left and then immediately turn right (the Heathland Trail continues to the left). Ignore a path on the left and go through a gate to reach the cricket ground. Go left and retrace your steps to the **Plough Inn**.

> **– To shorten**
>
> From the tower return to the big junction (Waypoint 3) and follow the Greensand Way to the small bridge over the River Tillingbourne and rejoin the walk at The Duke's Warren. This saves about 2km (30min).

Leith Hill Tower

At 313m the tower marks the highest point in south-east England. It was built in 1764–65 by Richard Hull of Leith Hill Place so his visitors could enjoy the views with small telescopes. After Hull's death in 1772 the building was neglected and fell into ruins. It was reopened in 1864 when a side tower was added to allow access to the top. The tower was given to the National Trust in 1923 and fully restored in 1984. You can visit the tower (entrance fee £3, or free to National Trust members). There is a small refreshment kiosk at the base of the tower.

Colley Hill is a perfect place to stop and enjoy the views

WALK 15
Reigate Fort

Time: 2½hr
Distance: 8km (5 miles)
Climb: 190m

Start/finish	*Reigate station*
Locate	*RH2 0BD ///shut.prop.corner*
Cafes/pubs	*Cafes, pubs and restaurants in Reigate*
Transport	*From M25 take A217. Trains from London*
Parking	*Car park in town centre or park along one of the minor roads*
Toilets	*No public toilets available*

A short climb followed by a gentle ridge walk with some interesting history along the way

This walk follows a section of the North Downs Way to Colley Hill and Reigate Fort, one of 13 forts built along the North Downs. Spend a relaxing afternoon on Colley Hill and allow some time to explore the fort before descending back to Reigate town.

The striking Inglis Memorial on Colley Hill

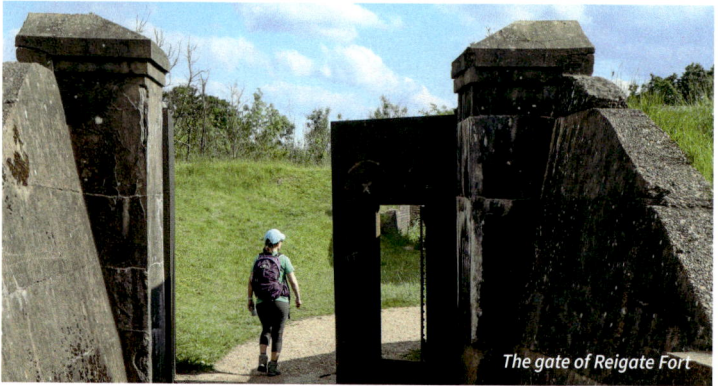

The gate of Reigate Fort

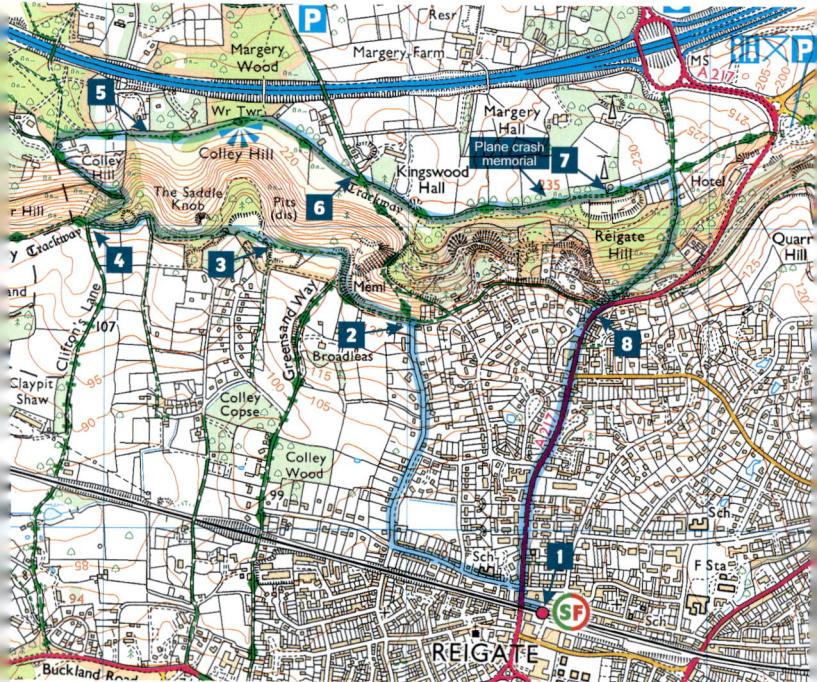

1 From the railway station go right on London Road (**A217**) then turn left onto Somers Road. A few minutes later go right on Pilgrims Way. Follow this road and at the end go left on a public footpath.

2 Follow the wide well-trodden path, ignoring any side paths. When the path splits, keep right following the North Downs Ridge Walk signs. Stay on the wide path bending slightly left. At a junction with the information board about the Colley Hill Hearthstone Mine go straight on along the North Downs Ridge Walk.

Hearthstone was a popular cleaning product used to whiten hearthstones and doorsteps in the 19th and early 20th centuries. The mine at Colley Hill operated from 1890 to 1961. During WW2 the mine tunnels were used as an air raid shelter.

3 Carry on through woodland, ignoring any side paths, and shortly climb some steps. At the top of the steps ignore a path joining from the right and continue straight on with the grassy hillside on your right. Follow the wide path through woodland, ignoring any unmarked paths.

4 At the junction with signposts go right uphill following the North Downs Way. Ascend on the wide path alongside a fence and follow the NDW to the right on the track by the first cottage. Follow the track for about 50m, passing some cottages, and then go right by the signpost. Walk alongside a fence following the NDW signs, ignoring any other paths.

5 Go through a gate and reach **Colley Hill**. Follow the prominent path with some great views of Reigate.

6 Pass the imposing, pillared Inglis Memorial, go through a gate and continue along the wide path. Soon pass a bunker and then a clearing with a **memorial to a plane crash**.

7 Shortly after arrive at Reigate Fort and explore the historic buildings. From the fort continue along the wide path, pass some houses and reach a junction. Turn right downhill leaving the NDW. When the path splits carry straight on downhill along the bridleway and a few minutes later arrive on the A217 road.

In 1898, with fears of a French invasion, 13 forts were built on the North Downs as part of the London Defence Scheme. The forts were meant to gather troops and supplies and slow down the French troops.

8 Turn right and follow the road back to the station.

— To shorten

At the end of Pilgrims Way go straight ahead at Waypoint 2 and climb Colley Hill. Turn right to rejoin the walk to the fort, saving about 3.5km (1hr).

Wing Tips

Part of the Wing Tips sculpture on Reigate Hill

On 19 March 1945, a B-17 'Flying Fortress' bomber crashed into the side of Reigate Hill, killing all nine crew members. The crash destroyed the trees on the hillside, creating a clearing. Today a pair of oak sculptures by sculptor Roger Day mark the crash site and commemorate those who died. The sculptures placed on each side of the clearing represent the aircraft's wing tips.

Clockwise from top left: the Surrey Hills offer visitors plenty of history; the North Downs Way traverses the Surrey Hills; the River Mole crosses the North Downs between Leatherhead and Dorking; bluebell carpeted forest floor; narrow path alongside grazing fields near St Martha's Hill

Lush vegetation along a narrow path (Walk 9)

USEFUL INFORMATION

Travel

Stagecoach www.stagecoachbus.com

South Western Railway www.southwesternrailway.com

Trainline www.thetrainline.com

Tourism organisations

The National Trust www.nationaltrust.org.uk

Surrey Hills Area of Outstanding Natural Beauty www.surreyhills.org

Visit Surrey www.visitsurrey.com

Surrey Wildlife Trust www.surreywildlifetrust.org

Accommodation

www.booking.com

www.airbnb.co.uk

© Nike Werstroh and Jacint Mig 2023
First edition 2023
ISBN: 978 1 78631 153 5

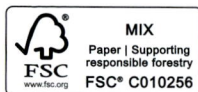

FSC
MIX
Paper | Supporting
responsible forestry
FSC® C010256
www.fsc.org

Printed in China on responsibly sourced paper on behalf of Latitude Press Ltd
A catalogue record for this book is available from the British Library.

OS
Map data

All photographs are by the authors unless otherwise stated.

CICERONE

Cicerone Press, Juniper House, Murley Moss, Oxenholme Road,
Kendal, Cumbria, LA9 7RL

www.cicerone.co.uk

Updates to this Guide

While every effort is made to ensure the accuracy of guidebooks as they go to print, changes can occur during the lifetime of an edition. Any updates that we know of for this guide will be on the Cicerone website (www.cicerone.co.uk/1153/updates), so please check before planning your trip. We also advise that you check information about transport, accommodation and shops locally. We are always grateful for updates, sent by email to updates@cicerone.co.uk or by post to Cicerone, Juniper House, Murley Moss, Oxenholme Road, Kendal, LA9 7RL.

Register your book: To sign up to receive free updates, special offers and GPX files where available, register your book at www.cicerone.co.uk.